CAPTAIN OF THE BIBLE QUIZ TEAM

Tom Jacobson

I0140055

BROADWAY PLAY PUBLISHING INC
New York
www.broadwayplaypublishing.com
info@broadwayplaypublishing.com

CAPTAIN OF THE BIBLE QUIZ TEAM
© Copyright 2017 by Tom Jacobson

Cover photos by John Perrin Flynn

First edition: May 2017
I S B N: 978-0-88145-697-4

Book design: Marie Donovan
Page make-up: Adobe InDesign
Typeface: Palatino
Printed and bound in the U S A

CAPTAIN OF THE BIBLE QUIZ TEAM was first produced by Rogue Machine Theatre (Stephanie Kerley Schwartz & Anna Nicholas, Producers) in Los Angeles, opening on 27 August 2016. The cast (in rotation) and creative contributors were:

PASTOR LANDRY SORENSON .... Amielynn Abellera
Wayne Tyrone Carr
Mark Jacobson
Deborah Puette

Director .... Michael Michetti
Costume design .... Stephanie Kerley Schwartz
Assistant costume design .... Megan Barker
Organist .... Barbara Browning
Ass't stage manager/Ass't director ...... Daniel Jordan Booth
Stage manager .... Daniel Coronel

CHARACTERS

LANDRY SORENSON, *a Lutheran minister*

The play takes place in the pulpit of a rural Lutheran church near Sauk Centre, Minnesota from December 2009 to April 2010.

Setting: A pulpit or lectern. A real church would be cool.

NOTES

Transitions are noted and are at the discretion of the director. Possibilities include simple lighting shifts, elaborate, choreographed costume changes (based on liturgical season), recorded musical interludes, or anthems by a live choir. The audience could be given hymnals and invited to sing seasonally appropriate hymns, or solos could by sung by a woman representing MRS DAHL.

When the audience members make reservations, they should be asked permission to have their names inserted into the play the night they are in attendance and asked to stand when their names are called. When they check in at the box office, they will be asked again to stand and remain standing when their names are spoken.

A MAN FROM AUDIENCE *will be invited to read a short scene from the script, and he should be alerted ahead of time and given the script page when he arrives for the performance. Preferably, he would be a fatherly sort. Or not. It might be fun to recruit a* WOMAN FROM AUDIENCE *instead for some performances.*

Two other AUDIENCE *members deliver notes to the pulpit during the performance. The first of these should be a* WOMAN FROM AUDIENCE, *the second could be of any gender. An audience member or someone from the theatre should also be recruited to rise when* DREW ZACZKOWSKI *is invited to stand.*

Pre-show music might have a Christmas theme.

SPECIAL THANKS

Pastor Joel Bergeland, Pastor James Bischoff, Pastor James Boline, Boston Court Performing Arts Center, Barbara Browning, Center Theatre Group, Pastor Caleb Crainer, Echo Theatre Company, Pastor David Eck, Bishop Guy Erwin, Pastor Ioan Ittu, Pastor Stephanie Jaeger, Lutheran Church of the Master, Pastor Andrew Nelson, Pastor Tyler Rasmussen, Pastor Robert Sterling Richards, Saint Matthew's Lutheran Church, Saint Paul's Lutheran Church, Pastor Peg Schultz-Akerson, Pastor Timothy Weisman, Pastor Peggy Yingst and David York.

(LANDRY, *a Lutheran minister wearing a clerical collar, appears in the pulpit. Some of the sermon is read aloud, other portions feel like improvisational riffs.*)

LANDRY: And it came to pass in those days that there went out a decree from Caesar Augustus that all the world should be taxed. And Joseph went from Galilee, out of the city of Nazareth into Judaea unto the city of David, which is called Bethlehem (because he was of the house and lineage of David) to be taxed with Mary his espoused wife, being great with child.

Merry Christmas! After the joyful anticipation of Advent, Jesus has arrived! We have much to celebrate tonight, much to thank God for. I haven't been here at Kandota Lutheran since my mother's funeral four years ago. And my presence tonight is almost as much of a surprise to me as it is to you. Bishop Bachhuber called just two days ago to tell me my father was in the hospital and wouldn't be able to lead the Christmas Eve service.

Dad would say it's "unsuitable" to tell you something this personal, but the doctors discovered a mass—not a Catholic mass, don't worry—in his abdomen and he underwent emergency surgery yesterday. I couldn't get a flight until today, so I haven't even spoken with him myself yet. He's starting chemo as soon as he's strong enough for that. I'll be taking care of him during his recovery, since—as you know—I'm an only child. Adopted, I think you also know, I mean, they couldn't—sorry! Unsuitable! I don't always do as my father says.

Another difference between me and my father is that I'm going to use sermon notes. I tend to get distracted or in trouble when I veer from prepared text. Yes, a pastor who makes mistakes! So:

When I dropped off my bags at the house—I found five Jell-O molds and bowls in the refrigerator, along with a list of names from Mrs Dahl, who kindly organized the, uh, Jell-O Festival. I'm delighted to thank each of the following for your thoughtfulness:

(Reads note)

Sue and Marvin Stoltenberg, orange Jell-O with carrot shreds

Pearl Huntsman, cherry with cherry pie filling—that was my favorite when I was a kid

Lois and Emil Doerr, lemon with pineapple and mandarin sections

Janet and Louise Speich, peach with raspberries

Karen and Wayne Olson, lime with cottage cheese, walnuts and onions

Thank you, all of you, and especially Mrs Dahl for letting everyone know.

I wrote most of these sermon notes on the plane from California, and as I thought about today's gospel reading I felt great kinship with Mary and Joseph on their journey back to his home town. We know Nazareth is eighty miles from Bethlehem, an arduous trip if you're nine months pregnant riding on a donkey. The donkey, by the way, isn't actually in the Bible—but it's hard to imagine a woman with a full-term pregnancy walking for five to seven days.

My trip wasn't so arduous—only one crying infant on my nonstop from Los Angeles to Minneapolis—but returning home is probably as profound for me as it was for Joseph. My father's Sorenson ancestors came to Minnesota from Norway almost a hundred and forty years ago, right around the time the church was founded as a Norwegian-speaking congregation: *Hvordan er du til i dag?* Sorry, that's all I know. But I've hundreds of Sorenson relatives in Kandota Township—many of you!

(Looks at congregation)

Most of you. I picked up the family genealogy research after Mom passed.

After I graduated high school—where I played the mellophone but did little else worth remembering, lots and lots of World of Warcraft—I'm kind of a geek—I went to college at Valparaiso, a good Lutheran school, where I majored in poli-sci. At Valpo I took a class in Hebrew, which led me to Aramaic, which led me to Greek, so before I knew it I was in graduate school in Berkeley, California, studying Biblical languages, plus Latin. That sounds like a path directly to the seminary, but God had other plans for me.

A graduate school friend invited me to go to Bolivia the next summer to volunteer for Fundación Arado. I learned quickly how different Bolivia is from Minnesota. Here we have Holsteins, Jerseys, Guernseys—in Bolivia they have llamas. They're God's creatures but nasty. They're also white, fluffy and kind of cute, so I wanted to get my picture taken with a llama I saw on a small farm. I posed next to it, my friend got the shot, and I started to walk away. Suddenly the llama reared up and wrapped its forelegs around my waist.

Lucky for me, the farmer ran up and shooed the llama away before it could—well, you know, we've all seen a bull on a cow—sorry!—unsuitable! I keep forgetting this is supposed to be a sermon. I confess to being a little nervous! And I did say I make mistakes. That was not the last, I promise you!

So…other than the llama thing, I loved Fundación Arado. We innoculated children, and most had never seen a needle before. One little girl named Nayra totally freaked out when she saw the other kids getting shots. Screamed, cried, carried on, so I said to her in my Google Translate Spanish: *por lo que no se enfermara*, this is so you won't get sick.

She stopped crying immediately.

Usted es Jesu Cristo? I laughed and told her, no, I wasn't Jesu Cristo, he died a long time ago. She started crying again: *Usted es Jesu Cristo! Usted es!* Like she'd been waiting for Jesus her whole life and wasn't about to have him snatched away. So finally I said *Si, Nayra. Soy Jesu Cristo.* I am Jesus.

Now you and I know that was very…unsuitable for me to say I was Jesus. But I realized that for Nayra, the typhoid innoculation was kind of a miracle. Typhoid kills thousands of Bolivians, especially children, every year. So for her, in that moment, I was Jesus. It was a shock. And a call. I applied to Pacific Lutheran Theological Seminary.

My pastoral internship at a church in Los Angeles— very urban, very diverse—ended more than a year ago, and I've been waiting for a call to a congregation ever since. I'm not alone in that—with the stock market crash last year, the economy in Kandota Township was hit especially hard, with hundred-year family farms forced into foreclosure—

Sorry…you're probably wondering what all this has to do with the gospel of the day. In seminary I had to take the Biblical Preaching course twice. My journey has only slight similarity to Joseph and Mary's—they were anticipating a birth and I'm—well—at least I'm not pregnant!

But I am grateful to be here. Back home. Even though I'd kind of given up looking for a call, especially in rural Minnesota—not that this is a call, I'm only authorized by the Bishop as a supply pastor until my

father can preach again. I'm not even ordained yet!
I won't be making pastoral visits in the turquoise
Volkswagen Beetle like my father—remember that
car? My best childhood memories were riding with
him farm to farm, the closest we ever were—sorry—
digression! But I do believe God called me here.
I'm grateful to the Bishop. I'm grateful to you. I'm
grateful for Jell-O. In fact—sorry this just occurred
to me, so maybe it's coming directly from God—
when you make Jello-O for somebody and fold in
raspberries—nuts—and cucumbers, you are emulating
Christ, you are Jesus, too. *Ustedes son Jesu Cristo.* Or, I
should say *Du er Jesus Kristus.* Jell-O may not seem like
much, but it's a great gift because it's the only thing my
father can eat right now.
Merry Christmas, indeed. *Feliz Navidad. God Jul!*
May the—uh—words of my mouth and the meditations
in our hearts be acceptable in thy sight, O Lord. Amen.

(Transition, possibly including Epiphany music)

LANDRY: And being warned of God in a dream that they
should not return to Herod, they departed to their own
country another way.
Does God still speak to us in dreams?
When I was eight Mom and Dad took me to Saint
Augustine, Florida so we could go swimming in
the ocean for the first time. The night before I had
a terrible dream that I was swallowed by a whale.
Was the dream a warning? From God? Sure enough,
my first time in the water I hit my head on a boogie
board and almost drowned. My father couldn't swim,
so he panicked, hollering for the lifeguard. When I
was brought to shore, the fear and love in Dad's eyes
terrified me. I'll never forget it. If you come to visit,
please don't tell him I told you—he'd hate that, deem it
unsuitable.

Before we explore our dreams together today, I want to thank everyone for your prayers for my father's health. He's been home a week, and the catheter should be coming out in a few days, which will be the signal that he's in good enough shape to handle the chemo. Back to dreams: imagine our little church, way out here in the country, deeply connected to the world beyond ourselves. I believe that's what God dreams for us. Which is why I'm delighted to announce our new collaboration with the Food Bank over in Sauk Centre. A number of our ladies have already joined in, contributing dry food stuff and canned goods— including many they canned themselves—like Arlene Gustavson's amazing rhubarb sauce. You know, it's almost impossible to get good rhubarb sauce in California.

I'd like to thank Drew Zaczkowski and our Our Lady of the Angels for inviting us to participate in the Food Bank. It's non-denominational, so it's okay. With the economy making it hard for some people to afford even the basic necessities, the mingling of crisp, green Lutheran pickles, Catholic cole slaw, Methodist applesauce and even Episcoreptilian canned sweet corn shows that churches are leading the way in time of trouble.

But you don't have to go all the way into Sauk Centre to join the fellowship of food. Today our traditional coffee hour in the church basement has grown into a little lunch (in California they'd call it brunch), with Mrs Dahl taking charge of Swedish meatballs. The only place you can get those in California is Ikea! Our dream is that this complimentary lunch will attract people who wouldn't ordinarily come to church, especially people suffering from the recession. In fact, I'm pretty sure I see a handful of new folks in the pews right now. Welcome! *Velkommen! Bienvenidos!* If Jesus could feed the five thousand, the least we can do is feed the people here today.

There is another dream we need to talk about today, a dream and a warning. My father has a dream for Kandota Lutheran, an ambitious dream for a Christian education building.

You can kind of see the foundation, concrete and studs, peeking out from under the snow between the church and the cemetery.

Arne Torkelson, our fine Church Council president, was kind enough to explain the mystery of that foundation, which has apparently been there, unchanged, for more than a year. You all know that your Council, faithfully helping my father realize his big dream, took out an equity loan on this property, the original church building and land. Unfortunately, due to the poor economy and declining offerings, the loan had to be used to fund annual operations. And we are very near default. For some of you this will be a great shock. It is for me. Dreams are wishes we hope will come true. My father's big dream has turned into a nightmare.

Traditionally, Kandota Lutheran has relied on a faith budget. We've always had faith that God would provide. But it should not shake our faith that the needed dollars have not appeared. God is giving us the opportunity to look beyond ourselves—

(LANDRY *notices a* WOMAN *approaching the pulpit.*)

LANDRY: Yes? Is something—? Oh, Mrs Dahl—!

(*The* WOMAN *places a note on the pulpit, then disappears back into the congregation [or perhaps leaves entirely].*)

LANDRY: Thank you! Should I—? It's a note.
(*Picks up note*)
(*Reads outside of note*)
"Please read." All right. Excuse me.

(Silently reads part of the note) I will read. Aloud. Yes? Is that what you'd like?

(No answer)

In any case, I believe this does bear reading aloud.

(Reads aloud)

"Since its reorganization in 1988 the Evangelical Lutheran Church in America has been obsessed with sinful sexual behavior, culminating in the acceptance of homosexual pastors last August at the 2009 annual churchwide assembly.

We have come to the conclusion that acceptance of deviant sexuality has finally replaced the Gospel of Jesus Christ as the foremost mission and message of the ELCA, which is jumping through theological hoops to twist the Bible into saying what they want, even when God so clearly says homosexuality is a sin. That means the ELCA is calling God a liar.

After prayerful consideration, we the undersigned are formally seeking dissolution of the relationship between Kandota Lutheran and the ELCA. We are taking this stand on behalf of ourselves and many others who wish to remain silent but also feel as we do."

This…um…you know, since this note was intended to be read aloud, I'm going to read the names. And I'm going to ask each of you to rise as your names are read. You have publicly taken a stand, and I hope you are willing to make that literal. So…

Mr Arne Torkelson, Congregation President

Mr and Mrs Marvin Stoltenberg

Mrs Lily Nilsson

Mr and Mrs Emil Doerr

Mr and Mrs Lowell Ellison Arlene Gustavson

Miss Janet Speich

Miss Louise Speich

Mr and Mrs Leif Sorenson
Mr and Mrs Wayne Olson
John, Teresa, Peter and Amy Flugstad
Ragnar Sorenson
Mrs Birgit Dahl
Reverend Ernest Sorenson
(He looks out at the congregation for a moment. It's unlikely that anyone has stood.)
Having just received this note—and this news—which is somewhat surprising as I've been in constant contact with congregational leadership for the last week and no one's said a word—I have no immediate comment.
(Big pause)
Well, yes, I do. In the five months since the 2009 adoption of the Social Statement: Human Sexuality, Gift and Trust, many individuals and congregations have begun the process of dissociation from the Evangelical Lutheran Church in America—the ELCA is indeed in crisis. But our church as a passive bequest to the next generation of Scandinavians and Germans—Lutheranism as lutefisk—isn't working—!
I apologize. You came to hear a sermon today, and that's not the one I was prepared to give. I was talking about dreams…
(Refers to sermon notes)
But perhaps God has other plans for us today. In fact, I'd like to call your attention to our Old Testament lesson, which has just become more pertinent than the gospel:
Isaiah 60: For behold, the darkness shall cover the earth, and gross darkness the people: but the Lord shall arise upon thee, and his glory shall be seen upon thee.
Storm clouds are most certainly gathering around us.
By now you've seen that I like to ask questions.
Sometimes, such as when I asked "what's that poking

out of the snow?" it gets me in trouble. But that's part of being Lutheran.

Martin Luther's large and small catechisms are structured on questions. He always asks "what does this mean?" And at the end of each answer, Luther reassures us "This is most certainly true." Luther's questions got us in a lot of trouble: the German Peasants Revolt, the Thirty Years War. Storm clouds gathered around our very founding.

But God was with us then and God is with us now. I will end today with one more question: if dreams are wishes, what is your dream for this congregation?

(Quickly)

May the words of my mouth and the meditations in our hearts be acceptable in thy sight, O Lord. Amen.

(Transition, possibly including music related to the Baptism of Jesus.)

LANDRY: And straightaway coming up out of the water, he saw the heavens opened, and the Spirit like a dove descending upon him. And there came a voice from heaven saying "Thou art my beloved Son, in whom I am well pleased."

Imagine this scene on the bank of the Jordan River, with Jesus midstream and his cousin John dunking him, then this voice booming down from heaven like Charlton Heston. As my father once said, "You can't have faith without imagination."

This riverside idyll represents the ultimate father/son relationship, a loving New Testament God bestowing his blessing upon a beamish boy. But not all parental relationships go this smoothly, as those of you who have ever been parents—or children—know. I now invite you to use your imagination once again as we dramatize another kind of familial scene, something a bit more Old Testament. I'd like to ask *(Name of a* MAN FROM AUDIENCE*)* to come forward at this time.

(MAN FROM AUDIENCE *comes forward carrying a script page.*)

LANDRY: And just so no one gets nervous, I want to reassure you these aren't real.

(He produces two glowing toy swords, one lit red, the other blue.)

I told you I was a nerd.

(LANDRY *meets* MAN FROM AUDIENCE *a few steps away from the pulpit and hands him the red sword.*)

LANDRY: Okay, take a deep breath.

(MAN FROM AUDIENCE *breathes.*)

LANDRY: Again! Louder! Slower!

(MAN FROM AUDIENCE *breathes.*)

LANDRY: Perfect! Now we need to spar a little bit.

(They fight. LANDRY *may make encouraging comments or otherwise direct the* MAN FROM AUDIENCE *in the fight.* LANDRY *may make light saber noises. Fairly quickly,* LANDRY *ends up on the floor with the* MAN FROM AUDIENCE *pointing the sword at* LANDRY'S *face.* LANDRY *gestures for the* MAN FROM AUDIENCE *to read from the script.)*

MAN FROM AUDIENCE: *(Reading from script page)* You have lost. Do not compound your foolishness or you shall surely die.

LANDRY: *(Reading from script page)* Noooo!

(LANDRY *jumps up and they fight.* MAN FROM AUDIENCE *cuts off* LANDRY'S *hand.)*

LANDRY: My hand! Noooo!
(Hides hand in armpit)

MAN FROM AUDIENCE: You have nowhere to turn. Do not force me to kill you. Come with me, and you will learn! Together, we can end this war and bring peace to the galaxy.

LANDRY: How can you imagine I'd come with you?!

MAN FROM AUDIENCE: They lied to you about the fate of your father.

LANDRY: I know enough! I know you killed him!

MAN FROM AUDIENCE: That is a lie. I am your father.

LANDRY: That couldn't possibly be true!

MAN FROM AUDIENCE: This is most certainly true.

LANDRY: Nooo! Nooo!

MAN FROM AUDIENCE: Come with me and we will rule the universe together!

LANDRY: *(Letting go and plunging down)* Nooooooo! *(He gets up.)*
Thank you. That was most excellent! I know it's not very Lutheran, but please give *(Name of* MAN FROM AUDIENCE*)* a round of applause!

(LANDRY gestures for MAN FROM AUDIENCE to return to his seat.)

(LANDRY returns to the pulpit, perhaps whistling a familiar John Williams theme as exit music for MAN FROM AUDIENCE.)

LANDRY: Now which of these father/son scenarios seems more familiar to you? Think about the great expectations God had for his son—saving the world by dying for its sins—and think about your own family, your father's expectations for you. Was he a loving, New Testament dad or a wrathful, Old Testament dad? My dad loves all of you like his children, but he loves me with…expectations. Long before I was in the picture, my Grandma Esther set those expectations. She prayed and prayed my parents would have a boy—a

beloved son—and that he would someday become
a Lutheran minister. Then I arrived. And gradually,
through Sunday School, confirmation, Luther Crest
Bible Camp and Luther League, I realized I wanted to
fulfill Grandma Esther's dream.

It wasn't a crazy expectation. On the wall of the church
basement—even today—you can see portraits of our
pastors since the early 1900s, several of them with the
last name Sorenson, many looking a lot like my father.
In our family, if you slit one wrist, lutefisk comes out,
slit the other and *A Mighty Fortress* plays.

I was proud to tell my father I wanted to follow in his
footsteps and go to seminary. His response was not
so much Charlton Heston as James Earl Jones, if you
know what I mean. Well, I'll tell you what I mean—he
said—oh, wait, hold on—wow—I apologize. I realize
you're probably all wondering how my dad's doing
this week since his set-back with the chemo. He's
improving. He's off the I V and can actually eat a little
something. So keep that Jell-O coming!

Which reminds me: a few of the ladies were asking
whether Jell-O is an appropriate contribution to the
Food Bank. Absolutely! But dry packages, not prepared
Jell-O with fruit and such.

We are expanding our Food Bank collaboration with
Drew Zaczkowski and Our Lady of the Angels, and
we will be honored as Church of the Week at Hope
Ministries in Saint Cloud next month.

Your generosity will reach beyond Kandota Township,
someday beyond the State of Minnesota, beyond the
United States, the planet Earth—our presence felt—
through God—in a galaxy far, far away. *Ustedes son
Jesu Cristo!*

But let's not neglect our home. I know everyone's
anxious about the equity loan crisis. I've been
sharing with the Council the tools I was exposed to

in seminary: strategic planning, stewardship drives, bequests and taxwise estate planning devices like charitable remainder annuity trusts.

We're not ready for all of that complicated stuff, and most of it won't help us in the short term.

But I've spoken to a handful of generous people— you know who you are but I won't embarrass you by naming names as you sit there in our pews— and we now have some very Lutheran anonymous commitments toward our loan repayment. Not yet enough to save us, but it's a start. You'll see shortly how all this relates to today's gospel, to the Baptism of Christ, the beloved son with whom His Father is well pleased.

We have complied with all ELCA requirements for today's special meeting to vote on termination of the relationship between Kandota Lutheran and the Evangelical Lutheran Church in America, which may also have implications for our equity loan challenge. This is a very serious vote. It's the most difficult situation I have ever encountered, including my mother's death and caring for my father these last two months. I know many of you feel the same. Several people have asked me what to do, some saying "Pastor, just tell us." I'm not going to do that, even though that's what you seem to be used to. I am not my father. I am not your father.

We are *God's* beloved children. Our eternal parental relationship is with Him, and He watches us as all fathers do, with both pride and worry. That's the good news of the New Testament, fatherly love transcending the wrath and punishment of the Old Testament. When we have the results of this vote—this most serious vote—will God be well pleased?

Let the words of my mouth and the meditations in our hearts be acceptable in your sight, O God. Amen.

(Transition, perhaps with Lenten music. By the end of the transition, LANDRY's *forehead is daubed with ash.)*

LANDRY: And when thou prayest, thou shalt not be as the hypocrites: for they love to pray standing in the synagogues and in the corners of the streets, that they may be seen of men. Verily I say unto you, they have their reward. But thou, when thou prayest, enter into thy closet, and when thou hast shut thy door, pray to thy Father which is in secret; and He which seeth in secret shall reward thee openly.

My Grandma Esther took this scripture literally, and when we visited as kids she went into her room and locked the door to do her daily devotions. As if prayer or faith were embarrassing or unsuitable for children. Before the service today, I was handed a note by—

(Looks out to confirm, nods)

—Mrs Dahl, who gave me permission to read it out loud.

(Reads from a note)

"Dear Fellow Faithful Lutherans: My family has seen the church through thick and thin for more than a hundred years, but since my husband Don's death and the cheating of the insurance company (a Lutheran insurance company, mind you), it is now Kandota Lutheran that is taking care of us. Thanks to your donations to the Sauk Centre Food Bank, my family has sufficient. And I am proud that together we have voted independence from the ELCA that has left God behind. As it says in Leviticus 20: If a man also lie with mankind as he lieth with a woman, both of them have committed an abomination: they shall surely be put to death. Yours in Christ, Mrs Birgit M Dahl"

(No longer reading)

Mrs Dahl, I congratulate you on your courage. I am personally grateful to you not only for acknowledging the generosity of this congregation, but also for your almost round-the-clock attention to my father in his illness. Thank you.

Although I am moved that you've chosen not to hide your light under a bushel, not to pray in your closet, I do have to make one clarification. Synod regulations require a second vote on the resolution to terminate. As you know, the vote was quite close last time, so the outcome is still very much in doubt. The next vote is scheduled just before Easter.

Tonight, Ash Wednesday, we enter into the contemplative period of Lent. God—and the ELCA's liturgical calendar—have given us an opportunity for self-reflection just when we most require it.

This being the end of my second month as your supply pastor, I will also use Lent as time for discernment. Most of my time, as you know, is spent here at church, at the Sauk Centre Food Bank, or at the hospital: my father's needs balanced with the needs of the church.

But, as one inquisitive and enterprising individual has observed, a few times a month I make the 100-mile drive to the Cities. Why would the pastor go all the way to Minneapolis so often, this person wondered? You have asked. I will tell.

Grandma Esther always dreamed we'd have another minister in the family, and ever since I was eight or nine, I wanted to follow in my father's footsteps. Dad's knowledge of the Bible is encyclopedic. Ask him why it's sinful to play football, and he will quote Leviticus 7 and 8: And the swine, of their flesh shall ye not eat, and their carcass shall ye not touch; they are unclean to you.

Throughout childhood, I was amazed by my father's wisdom, so I memorized the Bible. The entire Bible. I became Captain of the Bible Quiz Team, and led Kandota Lutheran to the Bible Quiz Nationals when I was a junior in high school. So I know that right after Leviticus 20, quoted by Mrs Dahl, there comes a chapter outlining the physical requirements for priests. They must not be "a blind man, or a lame, or he that hath a flat nose, or anything superfluous, or a man that is broken-footed, or broken-handed, or crookbackt, or a dwarf, or that hath a blemish in his eye, or be scurvy, or scabbed or hath his stones broken." Who among us is that unblemished? And yet Luther says we are all priests.

With Bible Quiz, Luther League, etcetera, I gave myself no time for the things teenagers normally do. Unlike some of my Sorensen cousins—and you know who you are—I never rode flat on the roof of the car going a hundred miles an hour on the U-Trail. I never skinny dipped at Fairy Lake. I was never in trouble. I was always in church.

In my third year at Valpo, I was hospitalized. The diagnosis: depression. I lost weight, I couldn't sleep. I was sent home for a semester. I don't think any of you knew that. I never left the house and my father said we couldn't tell anyone. What would we tell them? We didn't know what was wrong.

But that depression was a blessing. I think it came from God. It forced me to be quiet, to stop being the straight-A Captain of the Bible Quiz team. Forced me to listen. To myself. And, as it says in First Kings Chapter 19 Verse 12, to listen to that still, small voice of calm. I didn't really understand what the voice was saying, so I asked my father. His response: "Every family has its tragedy." He meant me. Who I am.

I went back to school, finished with a B average, went to grad school, volunteered in Bolivia, heard God's call, and entered seminary. When I told him I was going into ministry, my father stopped speaking to me. Well—no—because of something else he said, I stopped speaking to him.

With you I've been silent for two months, gave no personal testimony when we began the process to leave the ELCA over the Sexuality Statement. Facilitated our discussion, dialogue and vote without inserting my personal opinion. Why? Because I didn't want to influence your vote. Because I've always thought of Kandota Lutheran as my father's church. I loved it because it was his, because I loved him, despite his—disappointment—in me. I've been caretaking not only Dad but Kandota Lutheran. I could have kept on simply caretaking, but I...cared too much. And I've fallen in love.

In the past my romantic feelings have been vague, abstract, tamped down. The church was more important to me than anything...personal. Then suddenly, recently, lightning struck. There is no denying it. I am in love.

Now it all makes sense. My depression in college, my prayers to be a drug addict or an alcoholic (because those conditions can be cured), love songs on the radio made sense for the first time. I finally understood that still, small voice of calm—which by the way sounded like neither Charlton Heston nor James Earl Jones. It sounded exactly like Morgan Freeman, who said, "Enough. I made you. Get on with it."

I am not a tragedy.

May you be blessed hearing this sermon as I have been blessed preaching it.

(Transition, possibly including music related to John 13:34-35. LANDRY may be barefoot.)

LANDRY: A new commandment I give unto you, that ye love one another as I have loved you.

Tonight is called Maundy Thursday because of these words. It's a commandment spoken by Jesus on the night of the last supper, the night of his betrayal, the night he humbly washed his disciples' feet. In Latin the

word for commandment is *mandatum*, the antecedent of
our word mandate, and that has evolved into Maundy.
Jesus said many important things, but this is his only
commandment; love one another as I have loved you.
And you've followed it faithfully here at Kandota
Lutheran. We are feeding one another, sharing a meal
as Jesus did with his disciples, and the increasing
number of new faces we see every week means we are
feeding souls as well as bodies.

Another way you've shown love is to my father. Until
he went into hospice this week, your many calls, visits,
and gifts of food have been deeply appreciated. As
you can imagine, this is the hardest Holy Week of my
life, and you have all eased Dad's anxiety and mine
with your thoughtfulness, especially the ladies of the
congregation. *Ustedes son Jesu Cristo!*

Oh, speaking of the ladies and before I forget: I have to
apologize for asking Goodwill to pick up the Christmas
sofa in the basement. I remember taking naps on that
sofa when I was a kid, and the poinsettia print—faded
as it was in several places and threadbare in others—
was as much a part of my life as it was of yours. But I
was unaware of the sofa's early history, donated when
it was outgrown by the Thronson family seventeen
years before my birth then given new life by the ladies
who re-upholstered it in what was once vivid red and
green. I should have asked your permission before
making disposal arrangements, and I'm sorry for the
hurt it has caused. I promised you mistakes and this is
not my last! I am not unblemished! Let's imagine the
holiday sofa restuffed and cheering a family who has
less than ourselves.

Speaking of loving one another, I'd like to ask Drew
Zaczkowski to stand. Some of you know Drew from
our work with the Sauk Centre Food Bank.

(Drew *is the same sex as* Landry.)

LANDRY: The reason I asked Drew to stand isn't just our wonderful collaboration with the Food Bank, but also because—well—I mentioned at the beginning of Lent that I'd fallen in love. I've fallen in love with Drew. I could give you a litany of Drew's qualities, but that would be even more embarrassing and you know them already: kindness, thoughtfulness, generosity, intelligence. And patience. Lots of patience with me—that annoying Pastor who asks people to stand. Thank you, Drew, for being the embodiment of Christ's commandment, and for loving me. It's okay to sit now.

(DREW *sits.*)

LANDRY: As you all know, on Palm Sunday we had our second vote to leave the ELCA, which passed with more than two-thirds majority. A letter certifying our resolution has been sent to Bishop Bachhuber, and we now await the Synod's determination about our final financial obligation to the ELCA. We may also be required to give the Synod our church building as has been the case with some of the 243 other congregations that have severed ties in the eight months since the Sexuality Statement. And we are still in danger of defaulting on our equity loan, so we could lose our sanctuary that way. This is most certainly true.

As we think about Christ's commandment and his betrayal by Judas more than two thousand years ago, I'm very conscious that some of you feel betrayed. How could the Bishop have sent Kandota Lutheran a pastor attracted to persons of the same sex? I have asked myself that question as well. Here's what I can tell you:

After my internship in Los Angeles ended a year ago, I prepared my call paperwork. When I got to the question "Is there anything else about you that you feel it's important for the Synod to know?" I thought about

it a few days, then finally wrote: "I believe my life
partner could be a man or a woman."

The Synod asked me to redo the paperwork. "Don't
lie," they said, "Just leave that out. Don't lead with
your sexuality." I told them I was through praying
in my closet. You will never be called, the Synod told
me. Let a congregation get to know you slowly. We'll
make sure you're called to a safe church. A *safe church*.
Instead, God called me home. You'll notice the Synod
has never sent you my paperwork.

But there has been another betrayal. Just this week
my father told me he'd been in conversation with the
Bishop about terminating the relationship with the
ELCA even before the Churchwide Assembly last
August. As you may know—I didn't—my father and
the Bishop have conflicted many times over the years.
The Bishop knew I might fall in love with someone of
my own gender.

He also knew this congregation was planning to leave
the ELCA over the Sexuality Statement—and sent me
here anyway. You've been betrayed and I've been
betrayed. What a trick God and the Bishop have played
upon us! At least we have that in common.

I've been reminded, however, in the past few weeks
what we don't have in common, even though I grew
up here and napped on the Christmas sofa. A few
of you have stopped taking communion from me.
Although we have more people coming to services
now, I still notice when you don't come forward.

Wow. I just—sorry for the tangent, but I just flashed
on a memory from childhood. We've all had this
one. You're swimming in Sauk Lake or Fairy Lake,
spending a lot of time in the water, then you finally
come out. And someone screams. Because you're
covered with little bloodsuckers or even big leeches,
and you didn't notice because they actually anesthetize

you a little bit when they bite so you don't feel it. No sting. Polite, almost apologetic invertebrates. I don't know why I thought of that just now, sorry.

When I baptized little Kalee a few weeks ago, I heard that some people were asking if my baptisms were valid. Just so you know: the Bishop granted me full authority to perform baptisms, celebrate communion, and grant forgiveness, even though I'm not yet ordained. You can ask him. Some of you have.

I don't hear these questions and concerns from the people who have them. They come to me second-hand from the few people who voted against termination of our relationship with the ELCA.

There have been ugly words both public and private. Lifelong friends aren't speaking to one another. My own father refuses to even say my name.

What is most important here? Isn't it that we obey Christ's commandment to love one another, especially when we feel betrayed? Isn't that what you normally do, especially when you so generously feed our community? When you bring Jell-O to a dying man? *Ustedes son Jesu Cristo.* But lately you haven't been behaving like yourselves. We are a house divided against itself.

Normally we have the Exchange of Peace *after* the Offering, but I'm re-arranging the service today because I feel we need peace now. Please stand.

(Perhaps some audience members stand.)

LANDRY: I know it's out of order. We are all out of order. Please stand with me.

(LANDRY waits until all or most of the audience is standing.)

LANDRY: The peace of the Lord be with you.

(LANDRY pauses in case anyone gives the traditional response "And also with you.")

LANDRY: Please turn to the person next to you and offer them peace.

(LANDRY *goes into the congregation and shakes hands with many members of the audience, saying "The peace of the Lord be with you" or "God's peace" or "The peace of Christ be with you always" or "Peace be with you".*)

(*Transition, perhaps including Good Friday music based on Isaiah 53:1-6.*)

LANDRY: Tonight's homily will be brief, since our Tenebrae service is based on readings of the seven last Words of Christ. Tenebrae is Latin for "darkness" or "shadows," which is probably one of the reasons we've never done this service before. Traditionally, Latin hasn't…played well at Kandota Lutheran, but tonight our hearts are in shadow.

The fourth Word of Christ from the cross was *"Eloi, Eloi, lama sabacthani?"* In King James, that's translated from the Aramaic as "My God, my God, why hast thou forsaken me?" But in other gospel verses, Jesus uses another word for God: Abba, which is an intimate term for "father", some say more like "papa" or even "daddy". Jesus is feeling abandoned not just by God, but by his father.

My father died this afternoon at 2:37. It was not… peaceful. He…cried out…as one abandoned. I could not have…gotten through it…without the people who were there with us. Thank you, Drew. You held my hand—as my father snatched his away. He refused to look at me, at us. He turned toward the wall.

Thank you, Mrs Dahl. You gave my father comfort I couldn't bring myself to give. The morphine—peace—quieting his—his—fury—I guess is what you'd call it. You are a brave woman, a compassionate soul. We don't always—agree—even in that dire—and critical—moment—but you were right. I'm sorry I—oh, God—sorry—!

Back to the Bible. It's safer. Back to the words of Jesus.
"

Papa, why have you forsaken me?" is the only one of
the last seven sayings that takes the form of a question.
It's pretty Lutheran of Jesus and also very Jewish,
asking a question that begs to be answered. In his
catechism, Luther only asks questions for which he has
an answer. What answer is there for the question "Why
have you forsaken me?" I don't know.

It's in our Lutheran heritage to ask questions, but
in our Nordic D N A to suppress. Today we have
so many questions, but no one dares ask—it is—
unsuitable. Hard questions are…rude. And we are
nothing if not polite. Aggressively nice. When we
get angrier, we get *even more polite.* Sorry—back to
scripture—

In all four of the gospels Jesus says "you must lose
your life to save it." So odds are he actually said that,
as opposed to the many sayings attributed to Jesus that
were made up after the fact by the gospel writers. The
Jesus Seminar, a group of elite Biblical scholars who
study the sayings of Jesus, found that only eighteen
percent were likely to be his. That means ieghty-
two percent of the supposed words of Christ were
fabricated by someone else, decades or even hundreds
of years after his death.

Speaking of making stuff up, of inaccuracies, many
people in this room believe the literal truth of scripture,
and some of you reminded me of that after last night's
service. The oldest extant—that means existing—the
oldest extant versions of the gospels are from the
middle ages, and they differ from each other in more
than four hundred thousand instances. In other words,
mistakes: translation errors, copying errors, more than
the total number of words in the New Testament. The

Bible as the literal Word of God is a dream, a wish that hasn't come true.

How are we to have faith when the Word is— inauthentic? When our belief is based on something proven—literally proven—to be full of mistakes? In seminary we are taught answers to that question—the transformative power of paradox, the truthful human- ness of contradictions—but tonight I don't know.

I always have questions for God, but now my questions are for you:

A couple of generations ago, my great aunt Anna was kicked out of this church when she married an Episcopalian. Are we still like that?

When I went off to college, Grandma Esther said "I hope they don't make you room with a jigaboo." That remark came from a place where everyone looks the same to me, but you all know who's a stiff Swede, a mean German, a calm Dane, an angry Finn, a Norwegian with a junky farm, and who's—God help them!—Polish or Belgian Catholic, and drinking's all those Belgians know.

Remember that wall of pastor portraits in the basement? Privately—very privately—I call it a wall of shame, each male face whiter than the last.

Were I to stay here, eventually those portraits would follow the Christmas sofa, which, by the way, didn't go to Goodwill. They wouldn't take it. I took it to the dump.

How can we move forward if we refuse to change? If our most soul-searching controversy is what happened to a couch? I believe the church—this church—could be a force for the—betterment—of society. If not, what good are we? Are we simply here to preserve this debilitated institution like—like—like a limp, green pickle?

Why bother to withdraw from the ELCA when Kandota Lutheran is dying, literally dying? We are weeks away from foreclosure. The number of people at services is slightly higher in the last few months, but overall we're stagnant, pathetic. *This* is most certainly true.

This church isn't God's house where all are welcome. It's not a sanctuary. It's a place where the worst happens, where friend turns on friend, parent turns on child—

We didn't recite the Apostles' Creed tonight. Maybe you didn't notice. Anyway, it wasn't an accident. I left out our fundamental statement of faith because tonight the Creed feels like empty words. Words I no longer believe. And I don't think you do, either.

Where does that leave us? Without faith in God or one another? Abandoned by…our father? Abandoned, we now realize, long, long ago. Rejected—betrayed—!

I apologize for my anger—my inarticulate—it is uncomfortable, awkward, impolite. But I wouldn't be so angry if I didn't…love this stupid, stupid church so much.

What do we do now? Do we have any fucking idea? I don't know. I don't know.

No lo se.

(Almost like glossolalia, kind of scary)

No lo se. No tengo idea. Bendictus. Non scio. Den gnorizo! Den echo idea! Ani la iwde! Jeg vet ikke! Jeg har ingen ide! Nie wiem! Nie mam projecia!

(Stops, stricken)

Oh, shit…

(LANDRY abruptly leaves. Transition, perhaps with celebratory Easter music. As the transition concludes, LANDRY places a funeral urn on the pulpit or somewhere else prominent.)

LANDRY: Mary Magdalen stood without at the
sepulchre weeping, and as she wept, she stooped down
and looked into the sepulchre, and seeth two angels in
white sitting, the one at the head, and the other at the
feet, where the body of Jesus had lain. And they say
unto her, Woman, why weepest thou? She saith unto
them, because they have taken away my Lord, and I
know not where they have laid him.

And when she had thus said, she turned herself back,
and saw Jesus standing, and knew not that it was
Jesus. Jesus saith unto her, Woman, why weepest
thou? Whom seekest thou? She, supposing him to be
the gardener, saith unto him, Sir, if thou hast borne
him hence, tell me where thou hast laid him, and I will
take him away. Jesus saith unto her, Mary. She turned
herself, and saith unto him, Rabboni; which is to say,
Master.

This is my favorite story in the Bible. And probably
the least true. It only appears in the Gospel According
to John, which was written sixty to seventy years after
Jesus died, the last of the four gospels, and the one the
farthest from the actual events.

The earliest gospel, by the way, the Gospel According
to Mark, doesn't have a resurrection story at all. It ends
abruptly after "a young man" tells the women in the
tomb that Jesus has risen. But Jesus never re-appears.
This ending—a mere rumor of resurrection—disturbed
the early church so much that bogus verses were
added—everything after Mark 16 verse 8— to give the
story a happier ending.

My father, Ernest Sorenson, was pastor at Kandota
Lutheran for the entirety of his adult life. He was a
good man. Who with my mother saw fit to adopt an
abandoned infant and raise me in this church. I believe
he loved me very much, until I disappointed him
beyond all tolerance. I loved him even as we waged

silent war for years. A good man, but a hard man. Uncompromising to the last.

In seminary they warn pastors: don't stay so long at a church that the congregation starts confusing you with God. Don't stay too long.

My father baptized almost everyone in this room. He knew every single verse of the Bible. He had the personal authority of Charlton Heston. Not difficult at all to confuse him with God. Not difficult to buy into his dream and take out an equity loan that endangered this church. Did my father stay too long? Not long enough for me. Not long enough for us to…give our story a happy ending.

You can't have a resurrection without a death, which is why it's okay in the Lutheran church to hold a funeral on Easter Sunday. You must lose your life to save it.

Early this Easter morning I found my father's will. Apparently he revised it just a month ago. You knew that, Emil Doerr, you signed as witness.

In his final testament, Dad bequeathed our family home and surrounding quarter-section, the fallow remnant of my grandparents' farm, to Kandota Lutheran. If it can be sold promptly—even in this terrible economy—it will be enough to pay our equity loan and save the church. The remainder of my father's estate, he left to Mrs Dahl.

My name is not mentioned.

So what have I inherited from my father? His faith? Isn't that more important than material goods? I certainly didn't want the farm, even though it's been in our family since the 1870s. Isn't faith the finer thing? The greater gift? To hear the Lord gently say your name like Mary Magdalen heard in her moment of deepest despair? But faith is, in fact, what I have lost, and it would take a miracle to bring it back. Isn't that the worst admission a pastor can make?

When I told my father I'd been called by God to serve
the people of God, he said something even worse than
the obscene ravings, the curses—literal curses—he cast
upon me in the hour of his death. My father said, "You
will be destructive in ministry."
As we have seen, he was right. I have not been up
to this task. The after church lunches, the cajoling
of the congregation to contribute to the Food Bank,
the incremental growth in attendance—none of this
matters if I can't serve the spirit. At that I have failed. I
am destructive in ministry.
Therefore, I have decided this is my last sermon to you
as your pastor. My resignation will be effective at the
conclusion of this serv—

(The MAN *or* WOMAN *approaches the pulpit, proffering a
note.)*

LANDRY: Oh, no, not another note.

*(*LANDRY *reluctantly takes the note. The* MAN *or* WOMAN
goes back into the congregation. LANDRY *opens the note.)*

LANDRY: In celebration of what has apparently become
our tradition of interrupted sermons, I will read this
note aloud.
(Sighs, reads)
"After much prayer and anguish, we the undersigned
are rescinding our membership in Kandota Lutheran
Church. The controversy over the Sexuality Statement
and the vote to leave the ELCA has left us broken, our
beautiful church now hollow, heartless. We must start
over if we are to recover our relationship with God and
each other.
Next week we will meet in a living room, perhaps
the Sunday after in a barn. As you've reminded us,
our faith began in a barn two thousand years ago.
We will apply to the ELCA to start a new mission
congregation, one that welcomes everyone, loves

everyone, as Jesus did. As Pastor Landry does. We
like a pastor who makes mistakes, who is one of us,
needing and deserving God's love. So we humbly beg
Pastor Landry to be the first pastor of our new church.
Blessings in Christ—Drew Zaczkowsky—

(DREW *stands.* LANDRY *reads a list. It is a compilation of the
names of all the members of the audience at the performance.
As they have been asked prior to the performance, audience
members rise when they hear their name called. Perhaps
the entire audience will be standing by the end of the
list.* LANDRY *is overwhelmed, stares out at the standing
congregation.*)

LANDRY: I…don't know what to say. I don't know.

(Big pause)

Except—well—I do have something I wasn't planning
on sharing with you…but you are not who I thought
you were…five minutes ago. This morning—this
Easter morning and the day of my father's funeral—I
awoke from a dream. I was swimming in the Pacific,
and I could see my father calling for me from the rocky
shore. Suddenly—as can only happen in a dream—I
was surrounded by jellyfish. I had to get out of the
water. I had to get to my father, waving and shouting
from atop a rock. I swam, walked, staggered through
the jellyfish. I felt one burn my leg, then a sting on
my chest, more and more, until I was stung all over.
As I reached the shallow water, my father put his
arm around me and guided me up the pebbly beach.
Then we were in our old turquoise Beetle—he was
driving, me in a fetal position in the passenger seat in
unbearable pain but feeling hopeful because I knew—
dream logic—that we were on the way to the hospital.
My father stared straight ahead as he drove, didn't
look at me. But he said: Landry. He said my name.
Landry, remember, no matter what happens, I will

always be with you. Watching over you. Always. This is most certainly true.

END OF PLAY

www.ingramcontent.com/pod-product-compliance
Lightning Source LLC
Chambersburg PA
CBHW070037110426
42741CB00035B/2797